LOOK WRITE & REMEMBER

Letter Formation Practice Pages

52 Reproducible, Hands-On Lessons That Really Help All Children Visualize, Write, and Learn Each Letter of the Alphabet

BY SUSAN BRINDISE

SCHOLASTIC
PROFESSIONAL BOOKS

New York • Toronto • London • Auckland • Sydney
Mexico City • New Delhi • Hong Kong • Buenos Aires

To my parents, whose love
and encouragement made learning
my LIT's fun and easy!

Cover and interior design by **Holly Grundon**
Poster design by **Norma Ortiz**
Interior illustrations by **Rusty Fletcher**

ISBN 0-439-26586-x

contents

Welcome to
Look, Write & Remember!

"LEARN YOUR LIT'S, NOT YOUR ABC'S!" should be the new slogan for kindergartners and first graders. Letters comprised of vertical and horizontal lines, such as *l*, *i* and *t*, are learned before letters comprised of circles such as *a*, *b*, *c* or diagonal lines such as *x*, *y* and *z*. When learning letter formation, children notice the direction used to form the first stroke of the letter. In this book, letters with the simplest formation to learn—such as *l*, *i* and *t*—are presented first, because vertical and horizontal lines are easier to form than diagonal lines. So, *Learn Your LIT's!*

Think of the process involved when an infant learns to walk. Prior to walking, an infant learns to roll, crawl and kneel. These are the building-blocks for walking: rolling is easier to learn than crawling, and so on. Similarly, when teaching printing, the easiest letters to form should be taught first. Letters comprised of horizontal and vertical lines are the building blocks!

YOU'LL FIND TWO UNIQUE FEATURES IN THIS BOOK. The brain receives the feedback necessary to develop fine motor skills, such as printing, through the sense of touch. Tactile activities enhance the learning process and encourage success. Therefore, *finger-tracing activities* are incorporated into the worksheets in this book.

This book also features important *visual mnemonic devices*, such as a quarter moon for *c* and a basketball for *b*, to help children remember individual letter formation.

Pre-Writing Skills

The skills necessary to learn to write are called pre-writing skills. Use the worksheets (pages 6-7) to determine if children are ready to begin printing letters. They should be able to copy the various lines and shapes independently before beginning printing. They are presented in order of difficulty, as are the letter worksheets. Use this tool to inform your instruction.

Using These Pages
Here's what you'll find on each page:

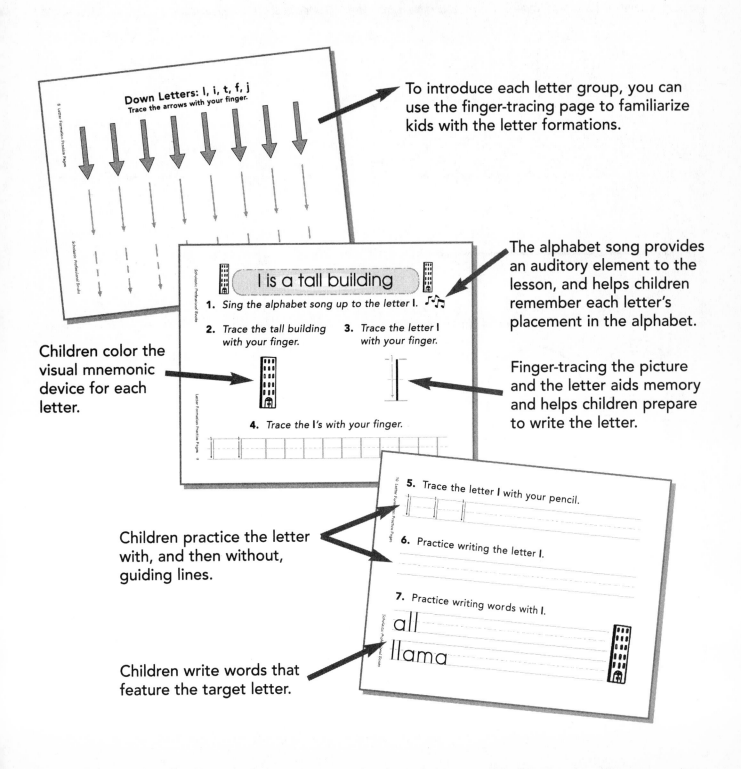

To introduce each letter group, you can use the finger-tracing page to familiarize kids with the letter formations.

The alphabet song provides an auditory element to the lesson, and helps children remember each letter's placement in the alphabet.

Children color the visual mnemonic device for each letter.

Finger-tracing the picture and the letter aids memory and helps children prepare to write the letter.

Children practice the letter with, and then without, guiding lines.

Children write words that feature the target letter.

Pre-Writing Worksheet

Copy each shape in the space provided.

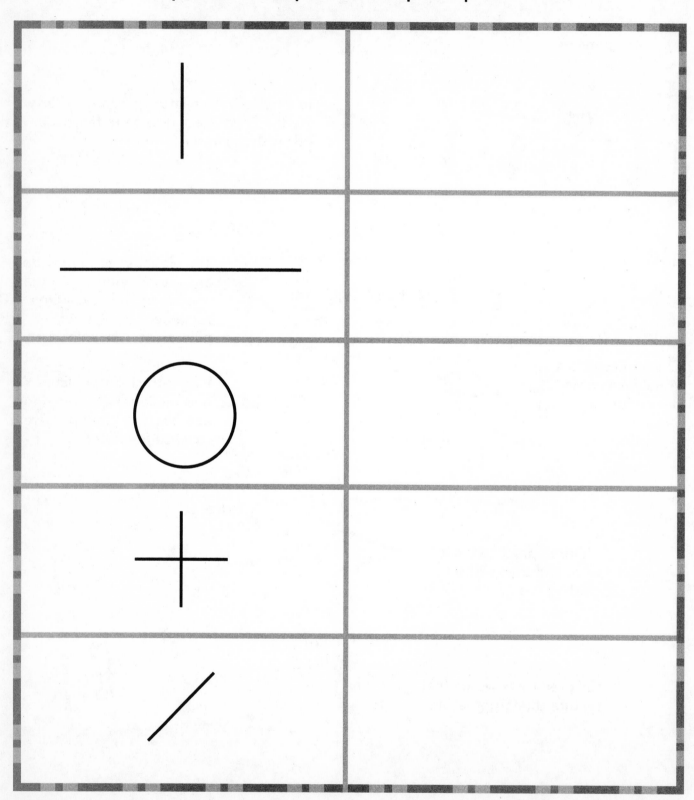

Pre-Writing Worksheet

Copy each shape in the space provided.

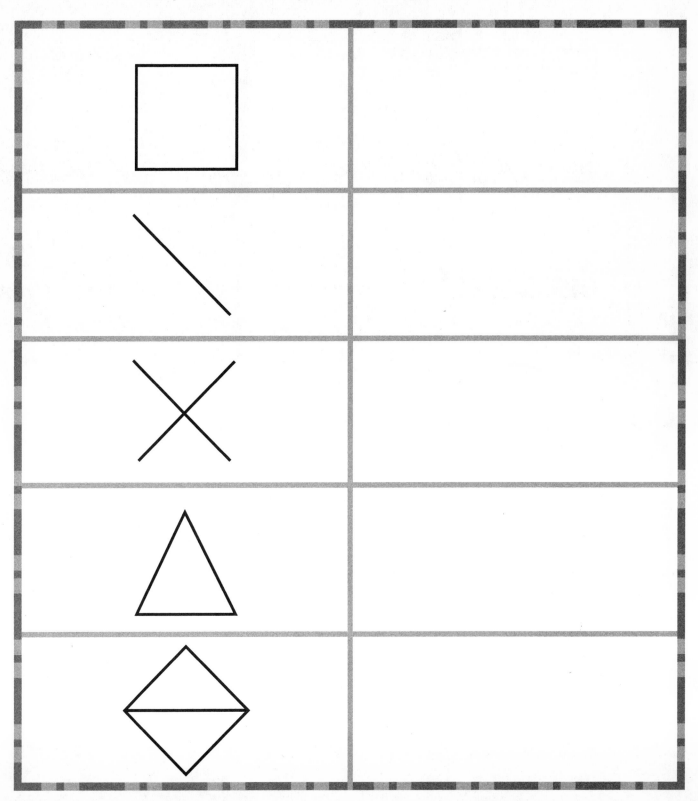

Down Letters: l, i, t, f, j
Trace the arrows with your finger.

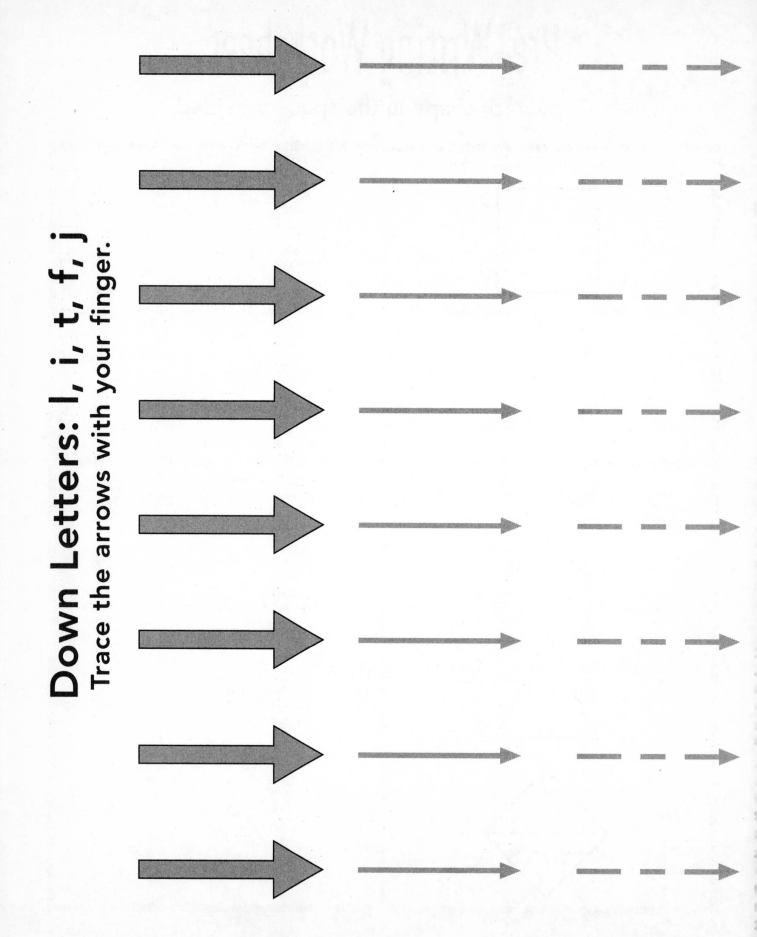

I is a tall building

1. Sing the alphabet song up to the letter I.

2. Trace the tall building with your finger.

3. Trace the letter I with your finger.

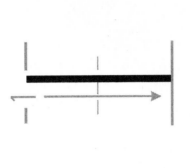

4. Trace the I's with your finger.

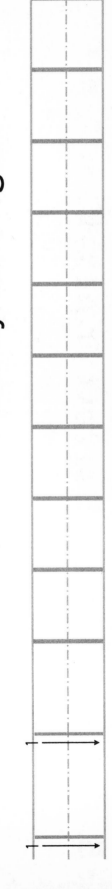

5. Trace the letter l with your pencil.

6. Practice writing the letter l.

7. Practice writing words with l.

all

llama

i is a candle

1. Sing the alphabet song up to the letter i.

2. Trace the candle with your finger.

3. Trace the letter i with your finger.

4. Trace the i's with your finger.

5. Trace the letter **i** with your pencil.

6. Practice writing the letter **i**.

7. Practice writing words with **i**.

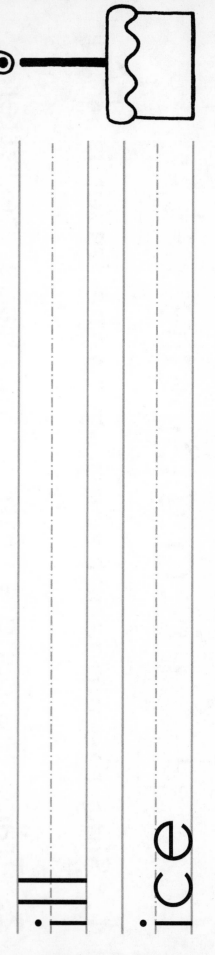

ill

ice

t is a totem pole

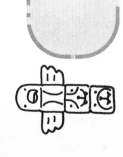

1. Sing the alphabet song up to the letter t.

2. Trace the totem pole with your finger.

3. Trace the letter t with your finger.

4. Trace the t's with your finger.

5. Trace the letter **t** with your pencil.

6. Practice writing the letter **t**.

7. Practice writing words with **t**.

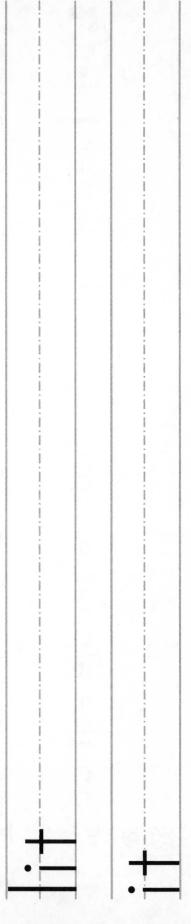

f is a candy cane with holly

1. Sing the alphabet song up to the letter **f**.

2. Trace the candy cane and holly with your finger.

3. Trace the letter **f** with your finger.

4. Trace the **f**'s with your finger.

5. Trace the letter **f** with your pencil.

6. Practice writing the letter **f**.

7. Practice writing words with **f**.

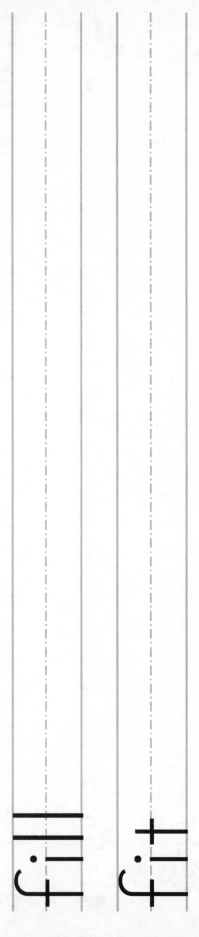

j is a candy cane and jellybean

1. Sing the alphabet song up to the letter j.

2. Trace the candy cane and jellybean with your finger.

3. Trace the letter j with your finger.

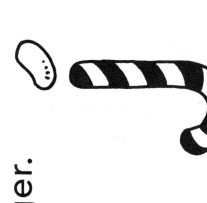

4. Trace the j's with your finger.

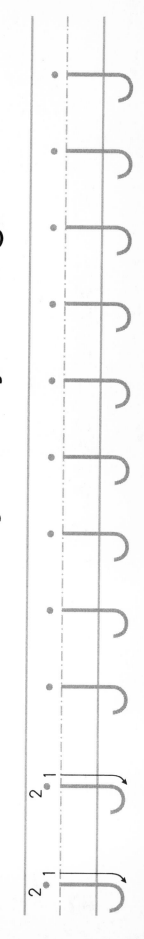

5. Trace the letter j with your pencil.

6. Practice writing the letter j.

7. Practice writing words with j.

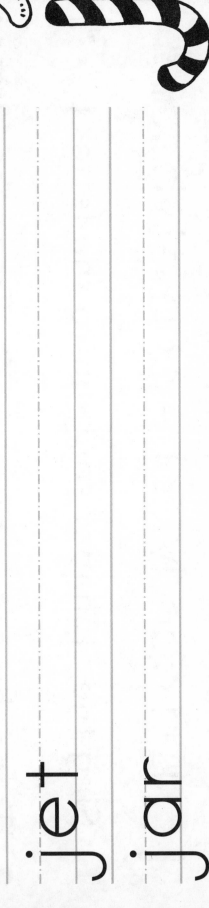

jet

jar

Practice printing the letters that go down.

Curves: n, h, u, s, m, r
Trace the arrows with your finger.

n is a barn

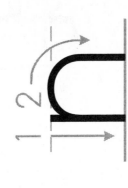

1. Sing the alphabet song up to the letter **n**.

2. Trace the barn with your finger.

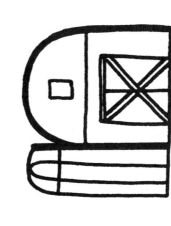

3. Trace the letter **n** with your finger.

4. Trace the **n**'s with your finger.

5. Trace the letter **n** with your pencil.

6. Practice writing the letter **n.**

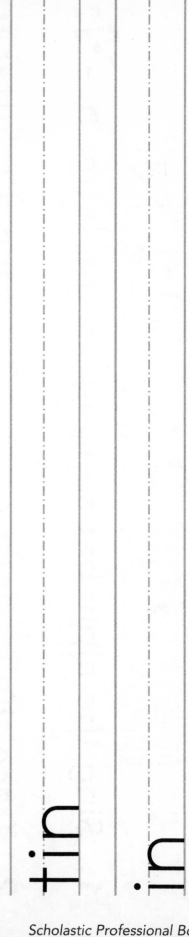

7. Practice writing words with **n.**

tin

in

h

h is a chair

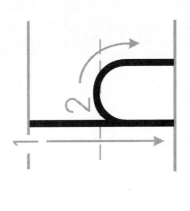

1. Sing the alphabet song up to the letter **h**.

2. Trace the chair with your finger.

3. Trace the letter **h** with your finger.

4. Trace the **h**'s with your finger.

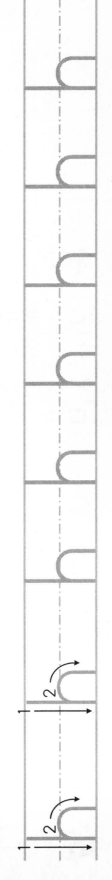

5. Trace the letter **h** with your pencil.

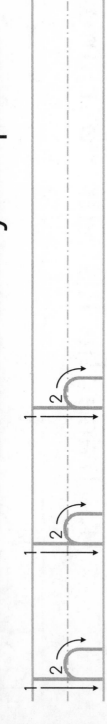

6. Practice writing the letter **h**.

7. Practice writing words with **h**.

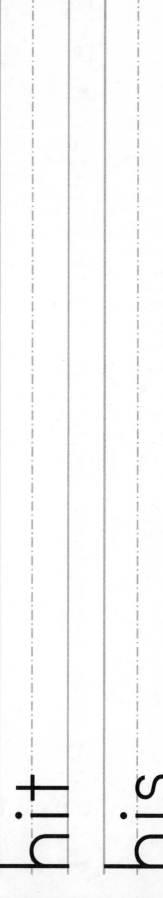

hit

his

  **u is a smile**

1. Sing the alphabet song up to the letter **u**.

2. Trace the smile with your finger.

3. Trace the letter **u** with your finger.

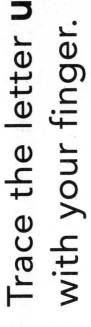

4. Trace the **u**'s with your finger.

5. Trace the letter **u** with your pencil.

6. Practice writing the letter **u**.

7. Practice writing words with **u**.

fun

nut

s is a snake

1. Sing the alphabet song up to the letter **s**.

2. Trace the snake with your finger.

3. Trace the letter **s** with your finger.

S

4. Trace the **s**'s with your finger.

S S S S S S S S S

S S S S S S S S

5. Trace the letter **s** with your pencil.

s s s

6. Practice writing the letter **s**.

7. Practice writing words with **s**.

is

sit

Scholastic Professional Books

 **m is a mountain**

1. Sing the alphabet song up to the letter **m**. ♪♫

2. Trace the mountain with your finger.

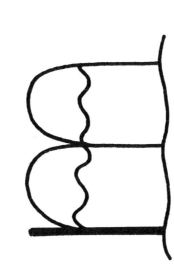

3. Trace the letter **m** with your finger.

4. Trace the **m**'s with your finger.

5. Trace the letter **m** with your pencil.

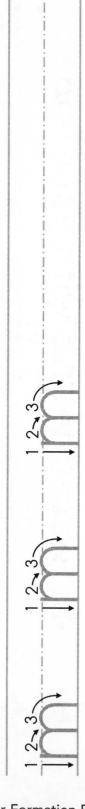

6. Practice writing the letter **m.**

7. Practice writing words with **m.**

hum

mitt

r is a faucet

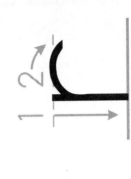

1. Sing the alphabet song up to the letter **r**.

2. Trace the faucet with your finger.

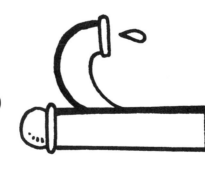

3. Trace the letter **r** with your finger.

4. Trace the **r**'s with your finger.

5. Trace the letter **r** with your pencil.

6. Practice writing the letter **r.**

7. Practice writing words with **r.**

or

rim

Practice printing the letters that curve.

Left Circles: o, d, c, q, e, a, g
Trace the arrows with your finger.

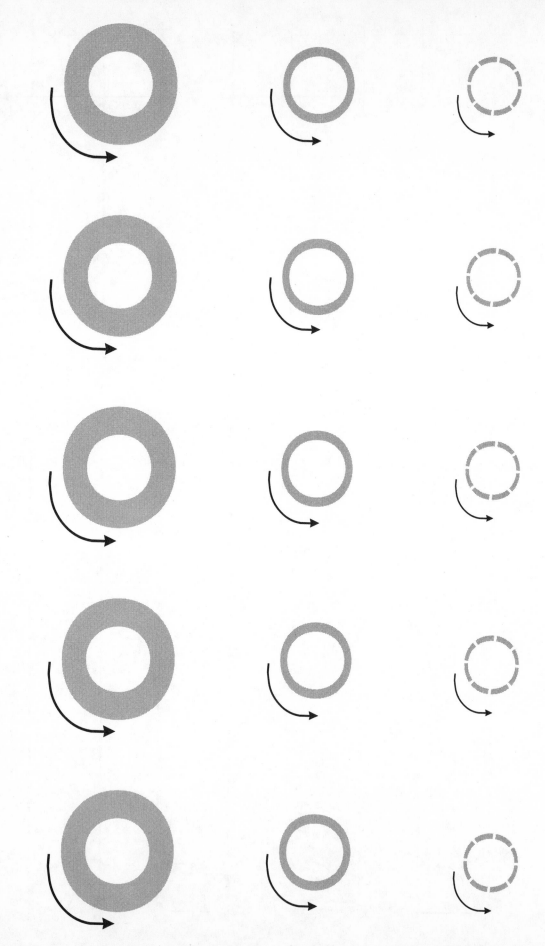

o is a moon

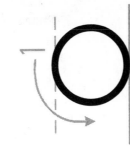

1. Sing the alphabet song up to the letter **o**.

2. Trace the moon with your finger.

3. Trace the letter **o** with your finger.

4. Trace the **o**'s with your finger.

5. Trace the letter **o** with your pencil.

6. Practice writing the letter **o**.

7. Practice writing words with **o**.

to

out

d is a moon and a line

1. Sing the alphabet song up to the letter **d.**

2. Trace the moon with your finger.

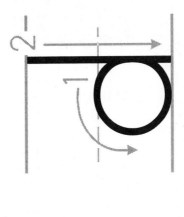

3. Trace the letter **d** with your finger.

4. Trace the **d**'s with your finger.

5. Trace the letter **d** with your pencil.

6. Practice writing the letter **d.**

7. Practice writing words with **d.**

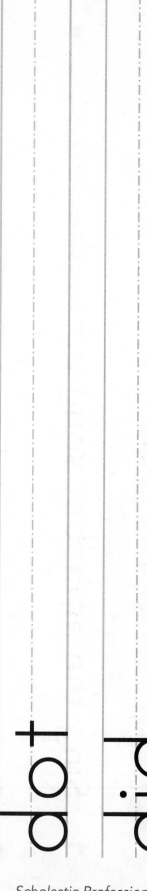

dot

did

c is a quarter moon

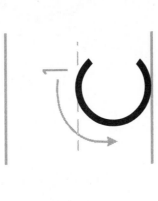

1. Sing the alphabet song up to the letter **c**.

2. Trace the moon with your finger.

3. Trace the letter **c** with your finger.

4. Trace the **c**'s with your finger.

5. Trace the letter **c** with your pencil.

6. Practice writing the letter **c**.

7. Practice writing words with **c**.

cat

cal

q is a moon and a line

1. Sing the alphabet song up to the letter q.

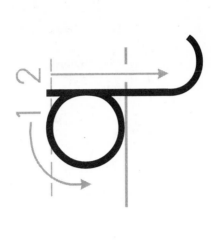

2. Trace the moon with your finger.

3. Trace the letter q with your finger.

4. Trace the q's with your finger.

5. Trace the letter q with your pencil.

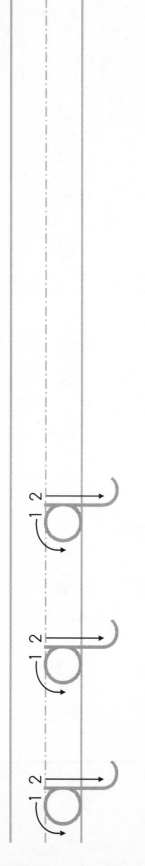

6. Practice writing the letter q.

7. Practice writing words with q.

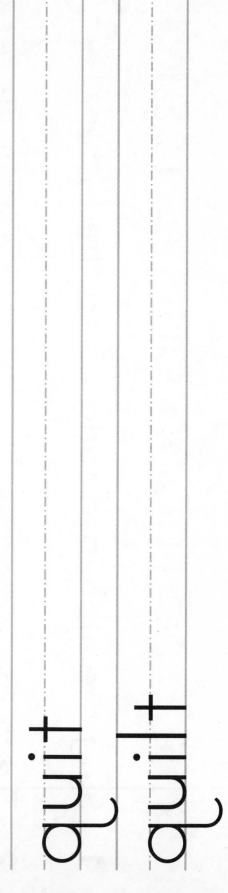

quit

quilt

e is a cloud, star, and moon

1. Sing the alphabet song up to the letter **e**.

2. Trace the cloud, star, and moon with your finger.

3. Trace the letter **e** with your finger.

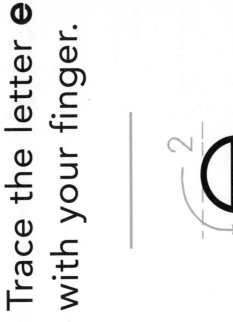

4. Trace the **e**'s with your finger.

5. Trace the letter **e** with your pencil.

6. Practice writing the letter **e**.

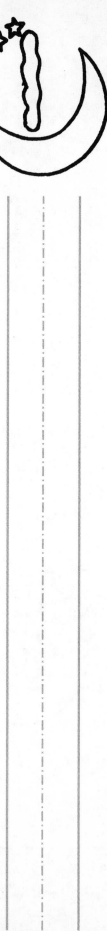

7. Practice writing words with **e**.

eat

egg

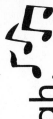 

a is an apple and a line

1. Sing the alphabet song all the way through.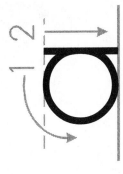

2. Trace the apple and line with your finger.

3. Trace the letter **a** with your finger.

4. Trace the **a**'s with your finger.

5. Trace the letter **a** with your pencil.

6. Practice writing the letter **a**.

7. Practice writing words with **a**.

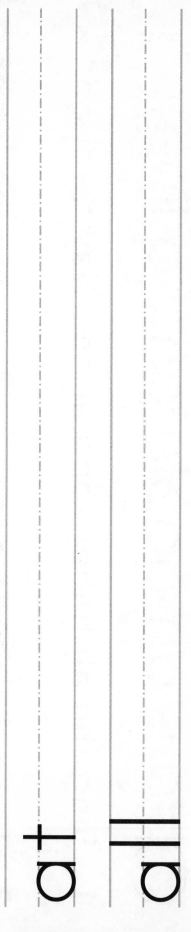

at

all

46 Letter Formation Practice Pages

g is a moon and a line

1. Sing the alphabet song up to the letter **g**.

2. Trace the moon and line with your finger.

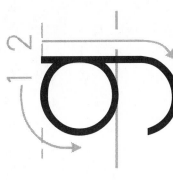

3. Trace the letter **g** with your finger.

4. Trace the **g**'s with your finger.

5. Trace the letter **g** with your pencil.

6. Practice writing the letter **g**.

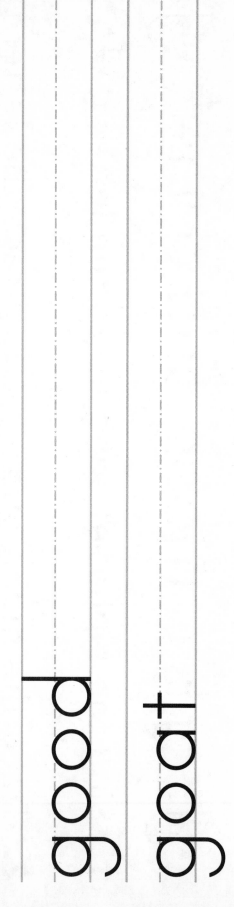

7. Practice writing words with **g**.

good

goat

Practice printing the letters that begin with a circle.

o o

a a

c c

d d

g g

Right Circles: b, p
Trace the arrows with your finger.

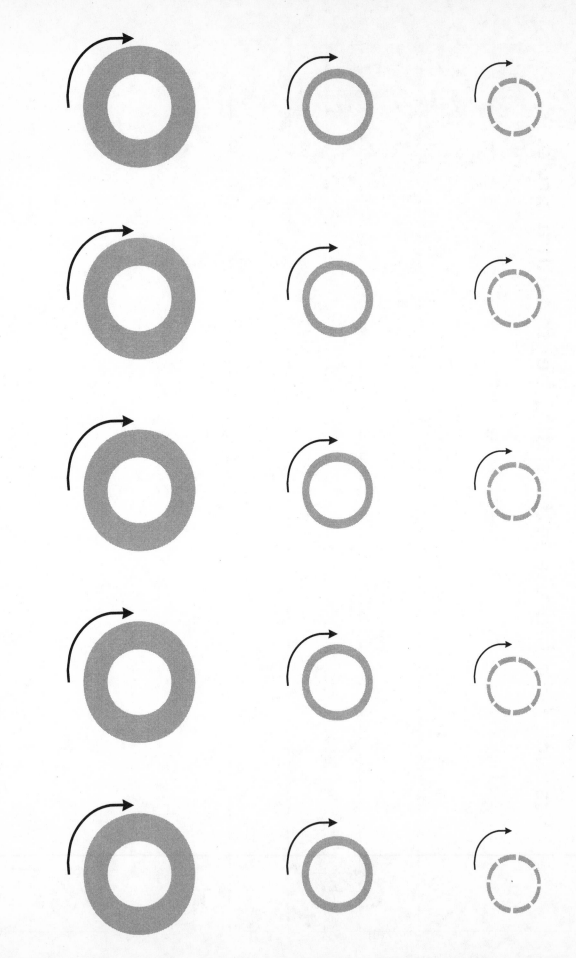

b is a basketball

1. Sing the alphabet song up to the letter **b**.

2. Trace the basketball with your finger.

3. Trace the letter **b** with your finger.

4. Trace the **b**'s with your finger.

5. Trace the letter **b** with your pencil.

6. Practice writing the letter **b**.

7. Practice writing words with **b**.

bat

ball

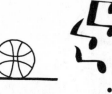 p is a ball and a line

1. Sing the alphabet song up to the letter **p**.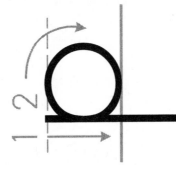

2. Trace the ball and line with your finger.

3. Trace the letter **p** with your finger.

4. Trace the **p**'s with your finger.

5. Trace the letter **p** with your pencil.

6. Practice writing the letter **p**.

7. Practice writing words with **p**.

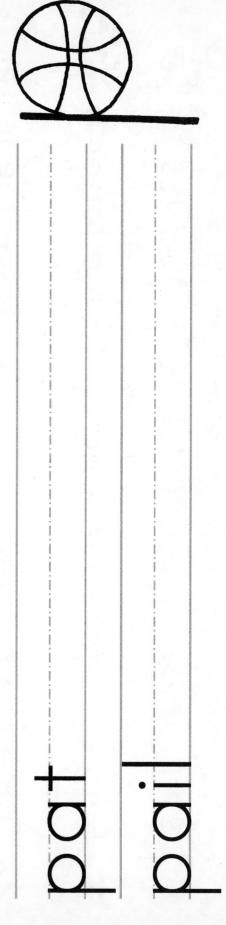

pat

pail

Scholastic Professional Books

Practice printing the letters that end in a circle.

Diagonals: v, x, k, z, w, y
Trace the diagonal lines with your finger.

v is an ice cream cone

1. Sing the alphabet song up to the letter **v**.

2. Trace the ice cream cone with your finger.

3. Trace the letter **v** with your finger.

4. Trace the **v**'s with your finger.

5. Trace the letter **v** with your pencil.

6. Practice writing the letter **v**.

7. Practice writing words with **v**.

vine

van

x is a railroad x-ing sign

1. Sing the alphabet song up to the letter **x**.

2. Trace the sign with your finger.

3. Trace the letter **x** with your finger.

4. Trace the **x**'s with your finger.

5. Trace the letter **x** with your pencil.

6. Practice writing the letter **x**.

7. Practice writing words with **x**.

ax

exit

Scholastic Professional Books

k is a karate kick

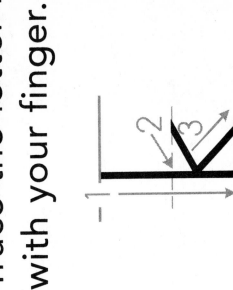

1. Sing the alphabet song up to the letter **k**.

2. Trace the karate kick with your finger.

3. Trace the letter **k** with your finger.

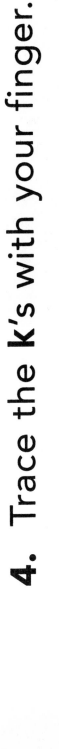

4. Trace the **k**'s with your finger.

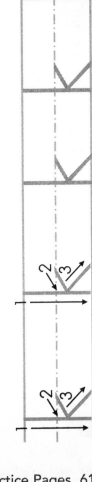

5. Trace the letter **k** with your pencil.

6. Practice writing the letter **k**.

7. Practice writing words with **k**.

kid

kite

z is a lightning bolt

1. Sing the alphabet song up to the end.

2. Trace the lightning bolt with your finger.

3. Trace the letter z with your finger.

4. Trace the z's with your finger.

5. Trace the letter **z** with your pencil.

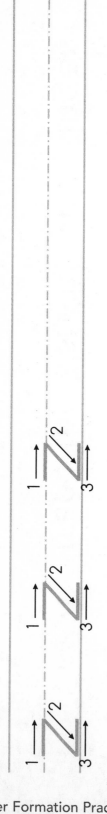

6. Practice writing the letter **z.**

7. Practice writing words with **z.**

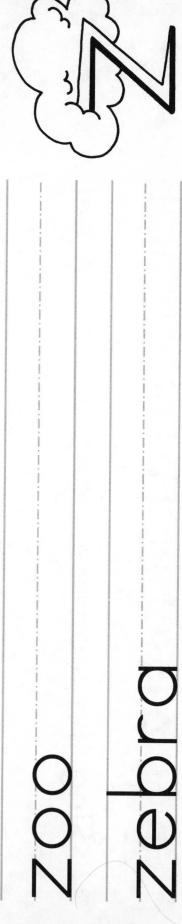

zoo

zebra

w is a crown

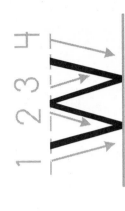

1. Sing the alphabet song up to the letter **w**. ♫

2. Trace the crown with your finger.

3. Trace the letter **w** with your finger.

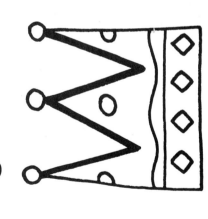

4. Trace the **w**'s with your finger.

5. Trace the letter **w** with your pencil.

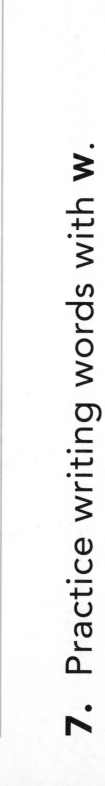

6. Practice writing the letter **w**.

7. Practice writing words with **w**.

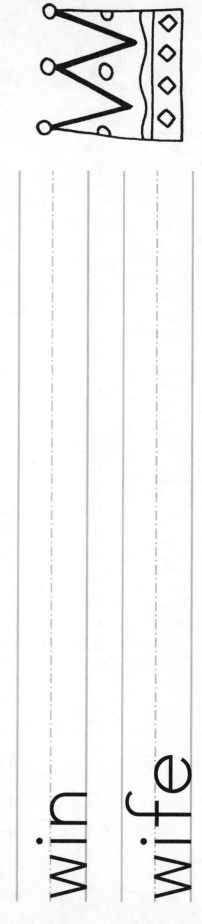

win

wife

y is a hand

1. Sing the alphabet song up to the letter **y**. 🎵

2. Trace the hand with your finger.

3. Trace the letter **y** with your finger.

4. Trace the **y**'s with your finger.

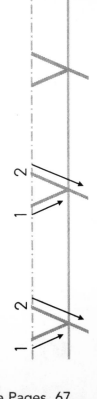

5. Trace the letter **y** with your pencil.

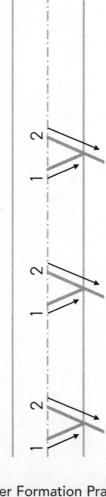

6. Practice writing the letter **y**.

7. Practice writing words with **y**.

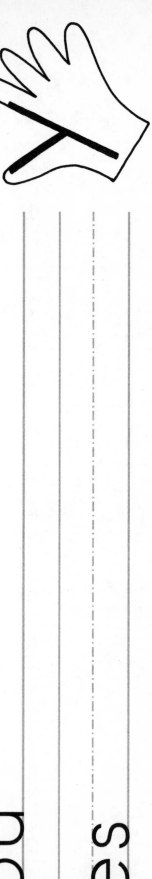

you

yes

L is a Golf Club

L is a down letter.
The first line you make goes straight down.

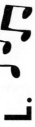 

1. Sing the alphabet song up to the letter **L**.

2. Trace the golf club with your finger.

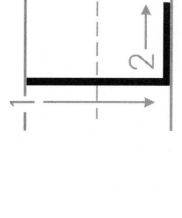

3. Trace the letter **L** with your finger.

4. Trace the **L**'s with your finger.

5. Trace the letter **L** with your pencil.

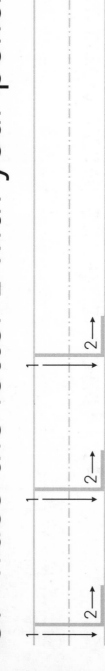

6. Practice writing the letter **L**.

7. Practice writing words with **L**.

Larry

London

T is a Hammer

T is a down letter.

The first line you make goes straight down.

1. Sing the alphabet song up to the letter T.

2. Trace the hammer with your finger.

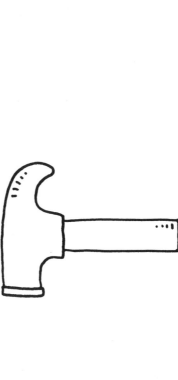

3. Trace the letter T with your finger.

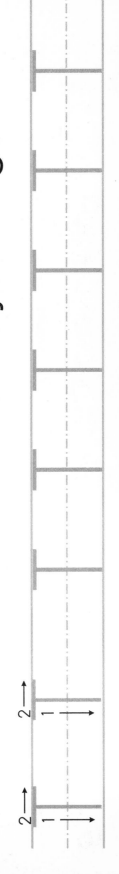

4. Trace the T's with your finger.

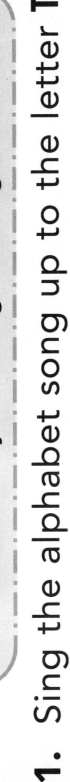

5. Trace the letter **T** with your pencil.

6. Practice writing the letter **T**.

7. Practice writing words with **T**.

Tom

Tina

J is a Candy Cane and Pencil

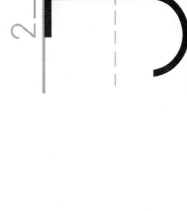

J is a down letter.
The first line you make goes straight down.

1. Sing the alphabet song up to the letter J.

2. Trace the candy cane and pencil with your finger.

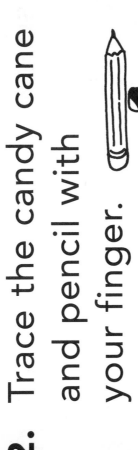

3. Trace the letter J with your finger.

4. Trace the J's with your finger.

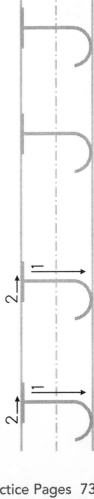

5. Trace the letter **J** with your pencil.

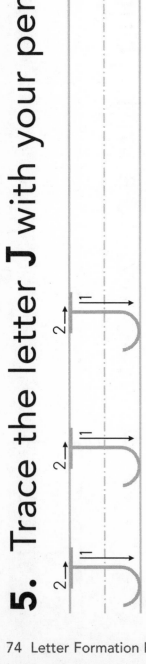

6. Practice writing the letter **J**.

7. Practice writing words with **J**.

Jim

Jenny

I is a Nail

I is a down letter.

The first line you make goes straight down.

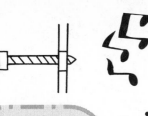

1. Sing the alphabet song up to the letter **I**.

2. Trace the nail with your finger.

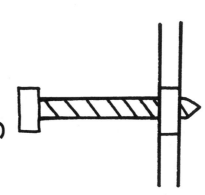

3. Trace the letter **I** with your finger.

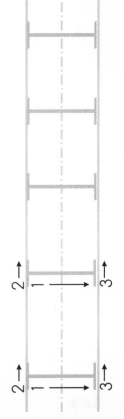

4. Trace the **I**'s with your finger.

5. Trace the letter **I** with your pencil.

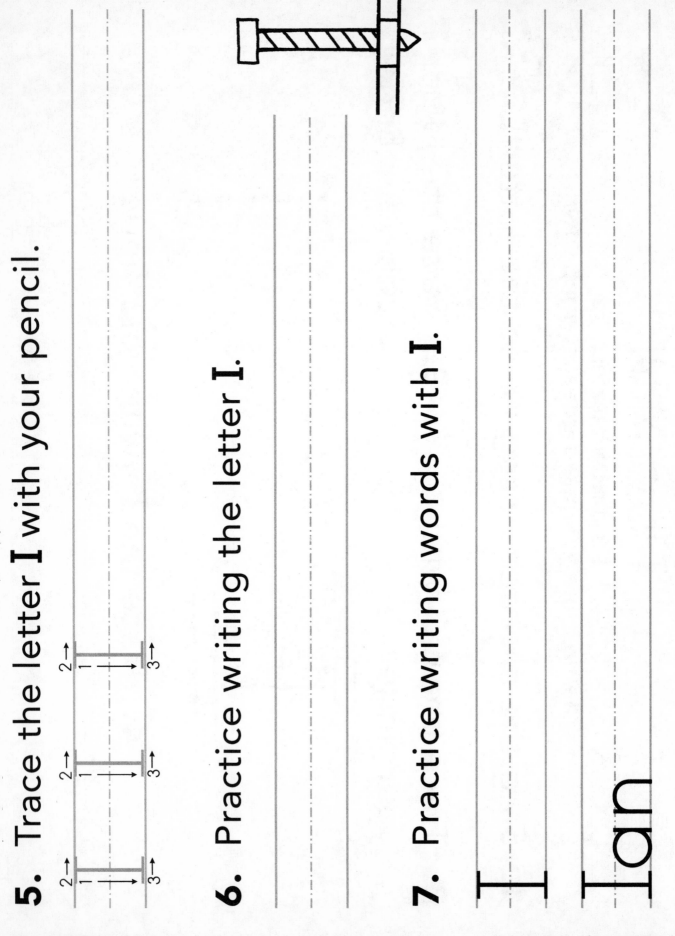

6. Practice writing the letter **I**.

7. Practice writing words with **I**.

Ian

F is a Flag

F is a down letter.

The first line you make goes straight down.

1. Sing the alphabet song up to the letter **F**.

2. Trace the flag with your finger.

3. Trace the letter **F** with your finger.

4. Trace the **F**'s with your finger.

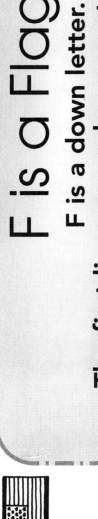

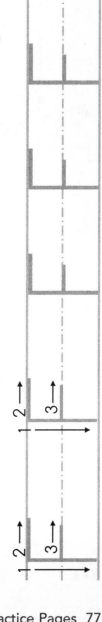

5. Trace the letter **F** with your pencil.

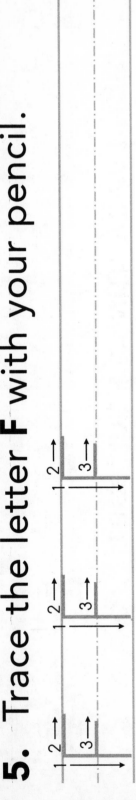

6. Practice writing the letter **F**.

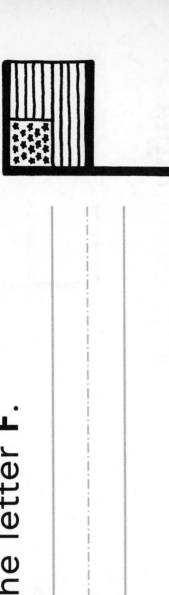

7. Practice writing words with **F**.

Fred

France

E is a Comb

E is a down letter.

The first line you make goes straight down.

1. Sing the alphabet song up to the letter **E**.

2. Trace the comb with your finger.

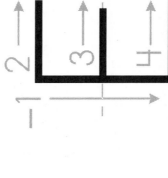

3. Trace the letter **E** with your finger.

4. Trace the **E**'s with your finger.

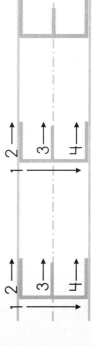

5. Trace the letter **E** with your pencil.

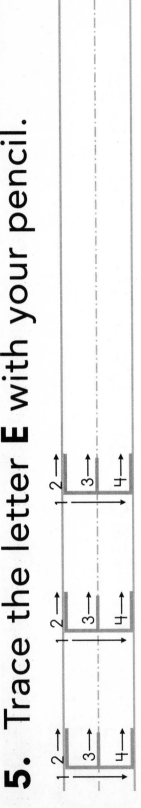

6. Practice writing the letter **E.**

7. Practice writing words with **E.**

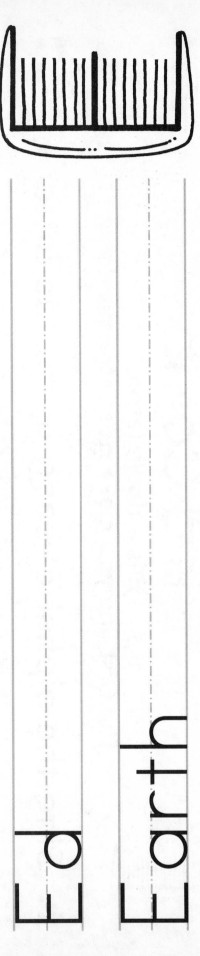

Ed

Earth

H is a Ladder

H is a down letter.

The first line you make goes straight down.

1. Sing the alphabet song up to the letter **H**.

2. Trace the ladder with your finger.

3. Trace the letter **H** with your finger.

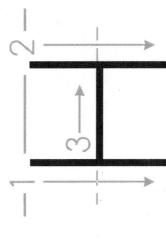

4. Trace the **H**'s with your finger.

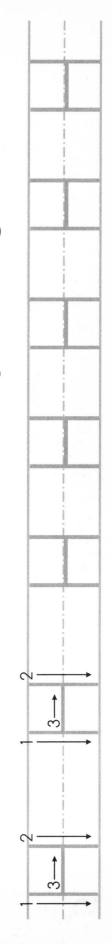

5. Trace the letter **H** with your pencil.

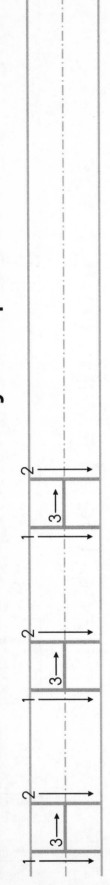

6. Practice writing the letter **H**.

7. Practice writing words with **H**.

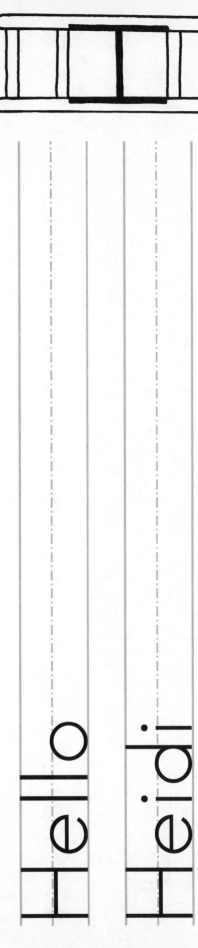

Hello

Heidi

82 Letter Formation Practice Pages

Down Letters

Practice printing the letters that begin with a down line.

Practice printing the letters that begin with a down line.

U is a Horseshoe

U is a curve letter. It has a curve.

1. Sing the alphabet song up to the letter **U**. 🎵

2. Trace the horseshoe with your finger.

3. Trace the letter **U** with your finger.

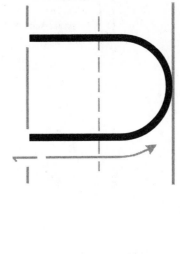

4. Trace the **U**'s with your finger.

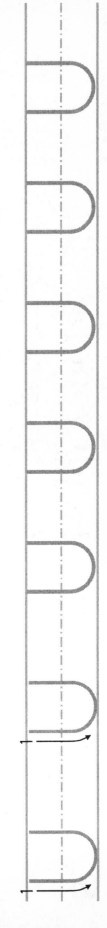

5. Trace the letter **U** with your pencil.

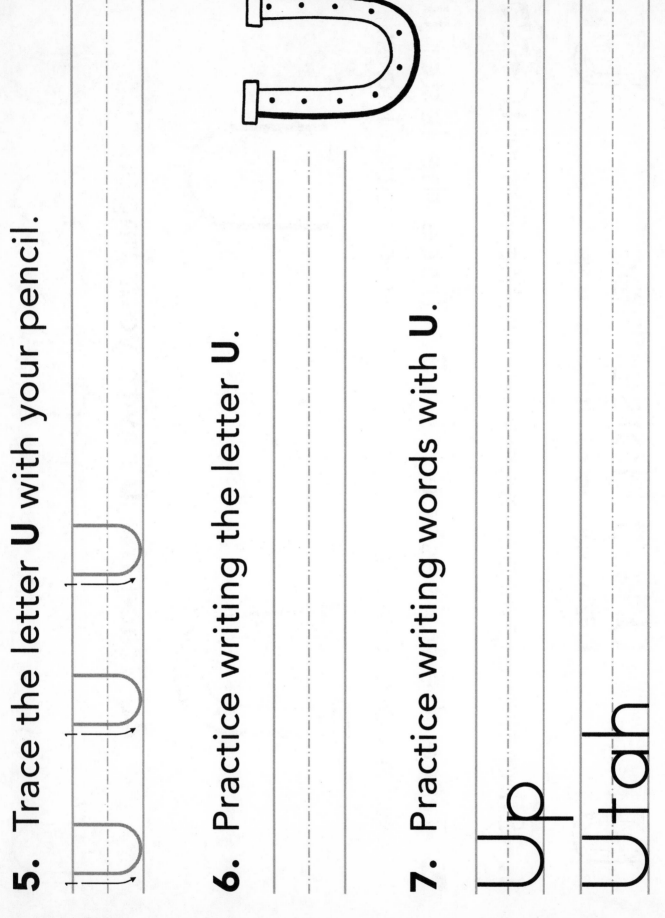

6. Practice writing the letter **U**.

7. Practice writing words with **U**.

Up

Utah

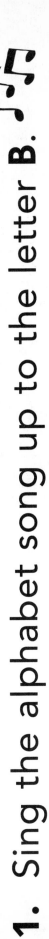

B is a Butterfly

B is a curve letter. It has a curve.

1. Sing the alphabet song up to the letter **B**.

2. Trace the butterfly with your finger.

3. Trace the letter **B** with your finger.

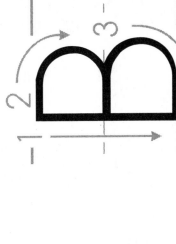

4. Trace the **B**'s with your finger.

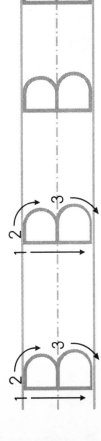

5. Trace the letter **B** with your pencil.

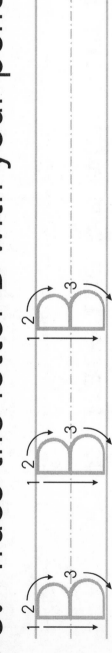

6. Practice writing the letter **B**.

7. Practice writing words with **B**.

Ben

Bill

Scholastic Professional Books

D is a Sailboat

D is a curve letter. It has a curve.

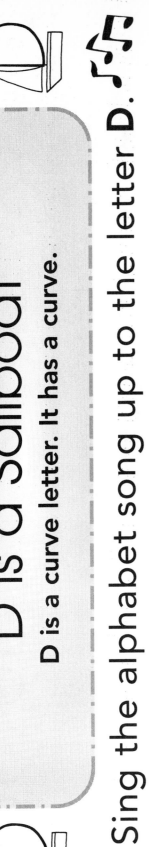

1. Sing the alphabet song up to the letter **D**.

2. Trace the sailboat with your finger.

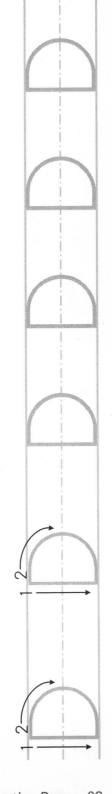

3. Trace the letter **D** with your finger.

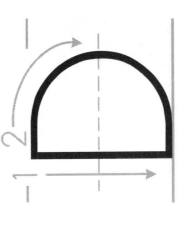

4. Trace the **D**'s with your finger.

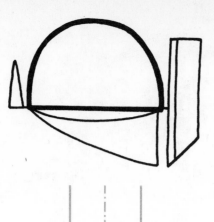

5. Trace the letter **D** with your pencil.

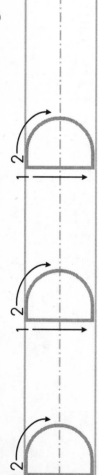

6. Practice writing the letter **D**.

7. Practice writing words with **D**.

Dan

Doctor

P is a Petal

P is a curve letter. It has a curve.

1. Sing the alphabet song up to the letter **P**.

2. Trace the petal with your finger.

3. Trace the letter **P** with your finger.

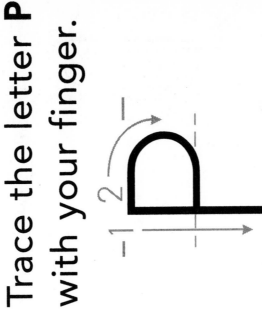

4. Trace the **P**'s with your finger.

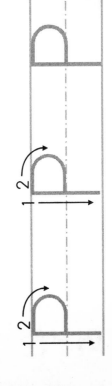

5. Trace the letter **P** with your pencil.

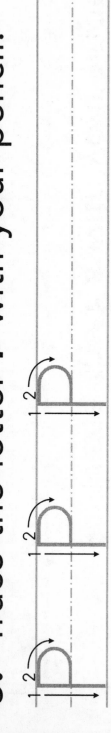

6. Practice writing the letter **P**.

7. Practice writing words with **P**.

Peter

Paul

S is a Snake

S is a curve letter. It has a curve.

1. Sing the alphabet song up to the letter **S.**

2. Trace the snake with your finger.

3. Trace the letter **S** with your finger.

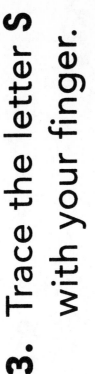

4. Trace the **S**'s with your finger.

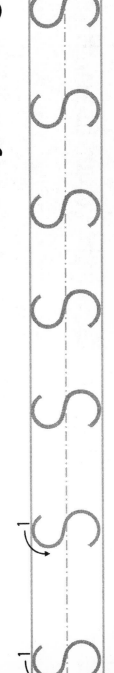

5. Trace the letter **S** with your pencil.

S S S

6. Practice writing the letter **S**.

7. Practice writing words with **S**.

Sam

Sean

Curve Letters

Practice printing the letters that begin with a curve.

U

B

D

P

S

Practice printing the words that begin with a curve.

BUD

SUDS

BUS

US

U.S.

Scholastic Professional Books

O is a Moon

O is a left circle. It starts with a backward circle.

1. Sing the alphabet song up to the letter O.

2. Trace the moon with your finger.

3. Trace the letter O with your finger.

4. Trace the O's with your finger.

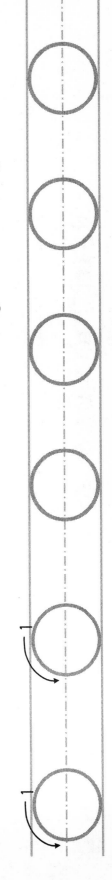

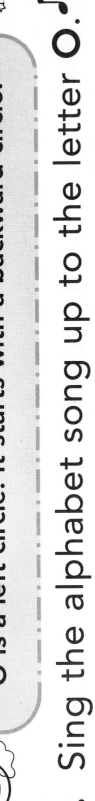

5. Trace the letter **O** with your pencil.

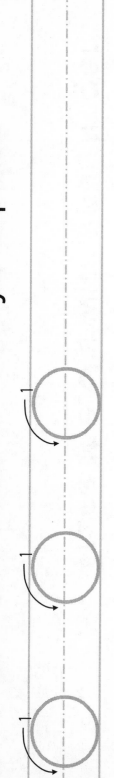

6. Practice writing the letter **O**.

7. Practice writing words with **O**.

Owl

Oliver

C is a Half Moon

C is a left circle. It starts with a backward circle.

1. Sing the alphabet song up to the letter **C**.

2. Trace the half moon with your finger.

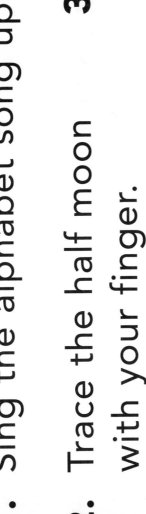

3. Trace the letter **C** with your finger.

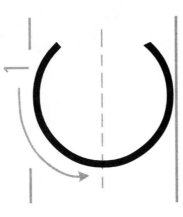

4. Trace the **C**'s with your finger.

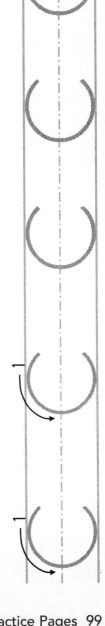

5. Trace the letter **C** with your pencil.

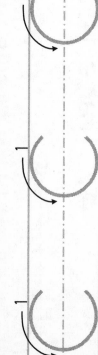

6. Practice writing the letter **C**.

7. Practice writing words with **C**.

Carrie

Canada

Scholastic Professional Books

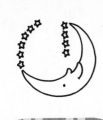

G is a Quarter Moon & Stars

G is a left circle. It starts with a backward circle.

1. Sing the alphabet song up to the letter **G**.

2. Trace the stars and quarter moon with your finger.

3. Trace the letter **G** with your finger.

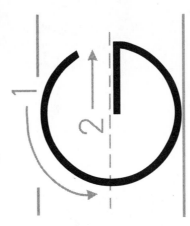

4. Trace the **G**'s with your finger.

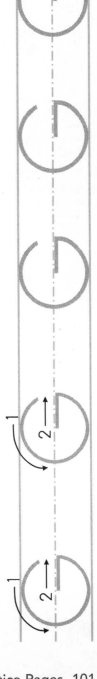

5. Trace the letter **G** with your pencil.

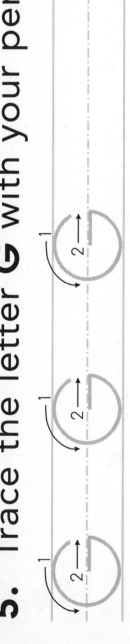

6. Practice writing the letter **G**.

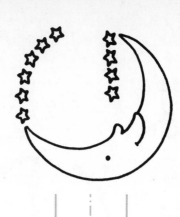

7. Practice writing words with **G**.

Gil

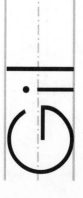

Greece

Scholastic Professional Books

Q is a Moon and Toothpick

Q is a left circle. It starts with a backward circle.

1. Sing the alphabet song up to the letter **Q**.

2. Trace the moon and toothpick with your finger.

3. Trace the letter **Q** with your finger.

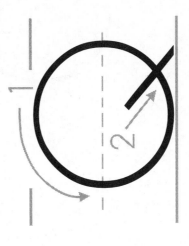

4. Trace the **Q**'s with your finger.

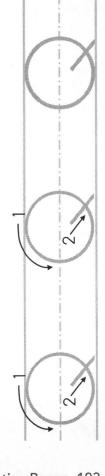

5. Trace the letter **Q** with your pencil.

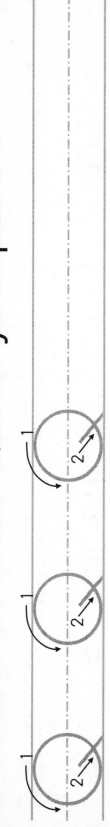

6. Practice writing the letter **Q**.

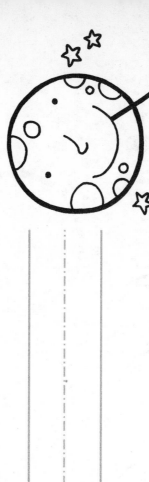

7. Practice writing words with **Q**.

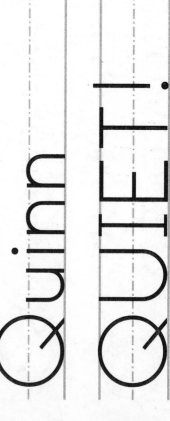

Quinn

QUIET!

Left Circle Letters

Practice printing the letters that begin with a left circle.

Practice printing the letters that begin with a left circle or curve.

CUB

CUP

GOB

BUG

GOOP

A is a House

A is a diagonal. It starts with a diagonal line.

1. Sing the alphabet song all the way through.

2. Trace the house with your finger.

3. Trace the letter **A** with your finger.

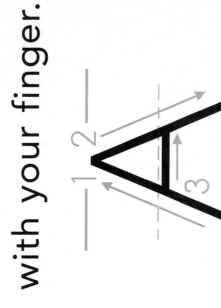

4. Trace the **A**'s with your finger.

5. Trace the letter **A** with your pencil.

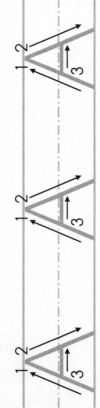

6. Practice writing the letter **A**.

7. Practice writing words with **A**.

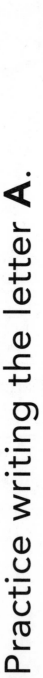

Amy

Arizona

V is an Ice Cream Cone

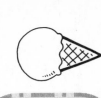

V is a diagonal. It has two diagonal lines.

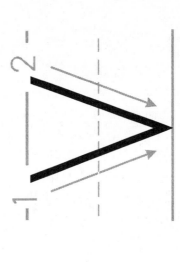

1. Sing the alphabet song up to the letter **V**.

2. Trace the ice cream cone with your finger.

3. Trace the letter **V** with your finger.

4. Trace the **V**'s with your finger.

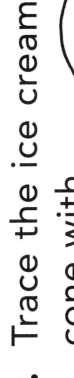

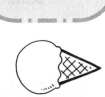

5. Trace the letter **V** with your pencil.

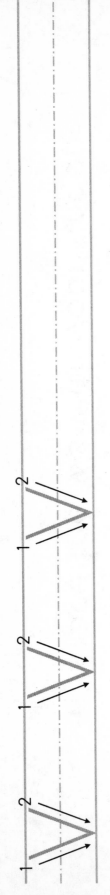

6. Practice writing the letter **V**.

7. Practice writing words with **V**.

Val

Vermont

Scholastic Professional Books

Z is a Lightning Bolt

Z is a diagonal. It has a diagonal line.

1. Sing the alphabet song up to the letter **Z**.

2. Trace the lightning bolt with your finger.

3. Trace the letter **Z** with your finger.

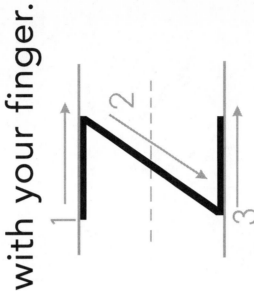

4. Trace the **Z**'s with your finger.

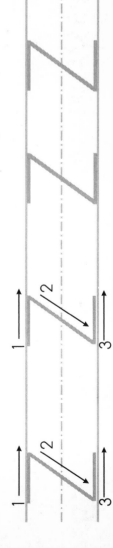

5. Trace the letter **Z** with your pencil.

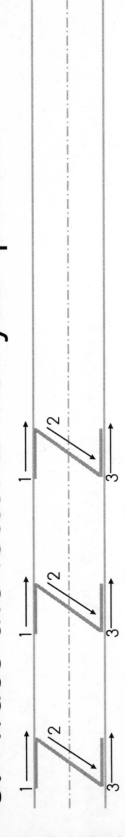

6. Practice writing the letter **Z**.

7. Practice writing words with **Z**.

Zoe

Zoo

M is a Mountain

M is a diagonal. It has 2 diagonal lines.

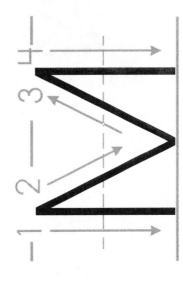

1. Sing the alphabet song up to the letter **M.**

2. Trace the mountains with your finger.

3. Trace the letter **M** with your finger.

4. Trace the **M**'s with your finger.

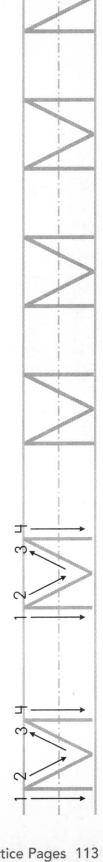

5. Trace the letter **M** with your pencil.

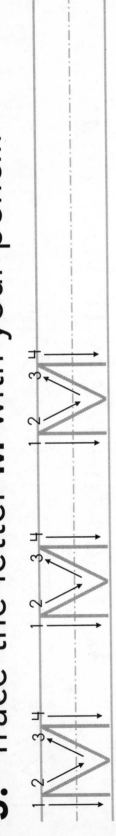

6. Practice writing the letter **M**.

7. Practice writing words with **M**.

Max

May

Scholastic Professional Books

R is a Man

R is a diagonal. It ends with a diagonal line.

1. Sing the alphabet song up to the letter **R**.

2. Trace the man with your finger.

3. Trace the letter **R** with your finger.

4. Trace the **R**'s with your finger.

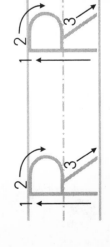

5. Trace the letter **R** with your pencil.

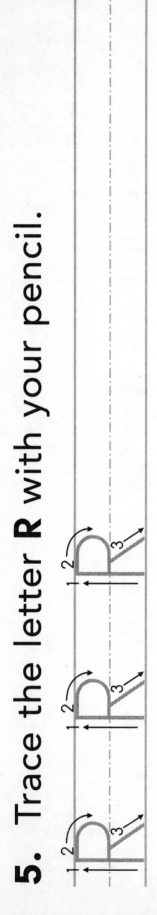

6. Practice writing the letter **R**.

7. Practice writing words with **R**.

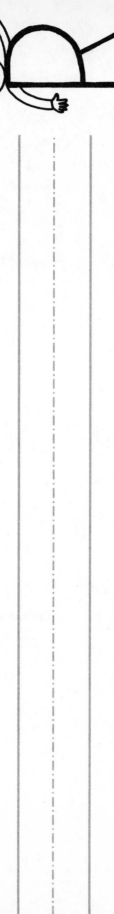

Rob

Ruth

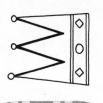

W is a Crown

W is a diagonal. It has four diagonal lines.

1. Sing the alphabet song up to the letter **w**. ♪♫

2. Trace the crown with your finger.

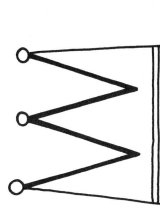

3. Trace the letter **w** with your finger.

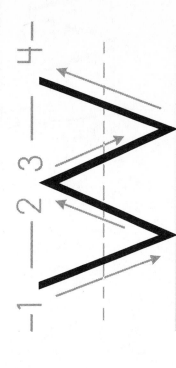

4. Trace the **W**'s with your finger.

5. Trace the letter **W** with your pencil.

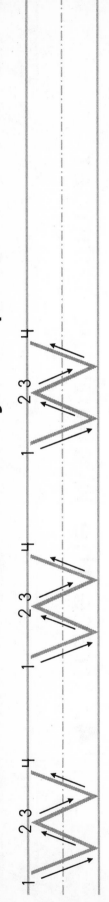

6. Practice writing the letter **w**.

7. Practice writing words with **w**.

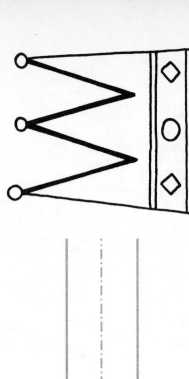

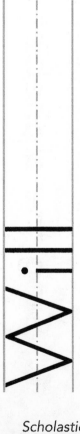

Will

Wyoming

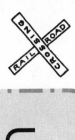

X is a Railroad X-ing Sign

X is a diagonal. It has two diagonal lines.

1. Sing the alphabet song up to the letter **X**.

2. Trace the railroad X-ing sign with your finger.

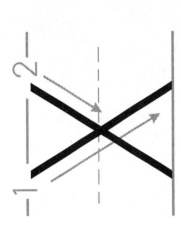

3. Trace the letter **X** with your finger.

4. Trace the **X**'s with your finger.

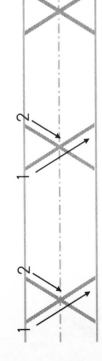

5. Trace the letter **X** with your pencil.

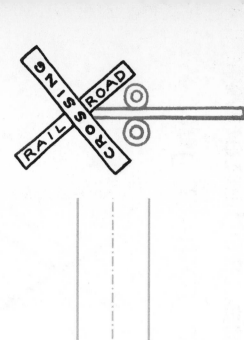

6. Practice writing the letter **X**.

7. Practice writing words with **X**.

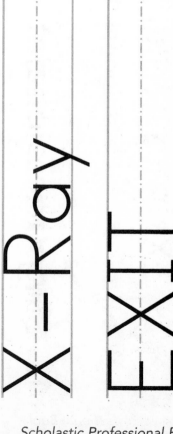

X-Ray

EXIT

N is a Nest

N is a diagonal. It has a diagonal line.

1. Sing the alphabet song up to the letter **N.**

2. Trace the nest with your finger.

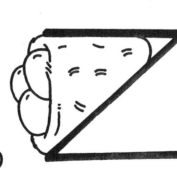

3. Trace the letter **N** with your finger.

4. Trace the **N**'s with your finger.

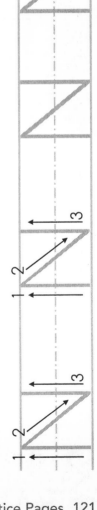

5. Trace the letter **N** with your pencil.

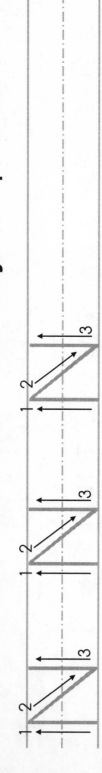

6. Practice writing the letter **N**.

7. Practice writing words with **N**.

Nancy

Nevada

Scholastic Professional Books

K is a Karate Kick

K is a diagonal. It has 2 diagonal lines.

1. Sing the alphabet song up to the letter **K**.

2. Trace the karate kick with your finger.

3. Trace the letter **K** with your finger.

4. Trace the **K**'s with your finger.

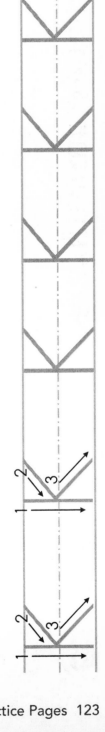

5. Trace the letter **K** with your pencil.

6. Practice writing the letter **K**.

7. Practice writing words with **K**.

Ken

Kansas

Y is a Tree

Y is a diagonal. It has two diagonal lines.

1. Sing the alphabet song up to the letter Y.

2. Trace the tree with your finger.

3. Trace the letter Y with your finger.

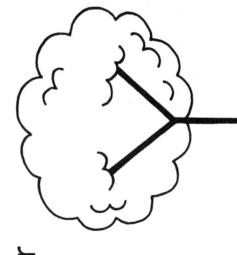

4. Trace the Y's with your finger.

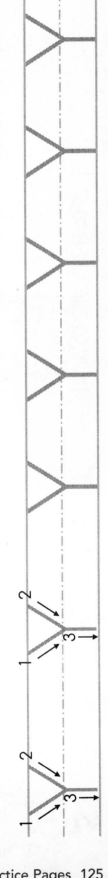

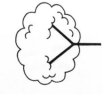

5. Trace the letter **Y** with your pencil.

6. Practice writing the letter **Y**.

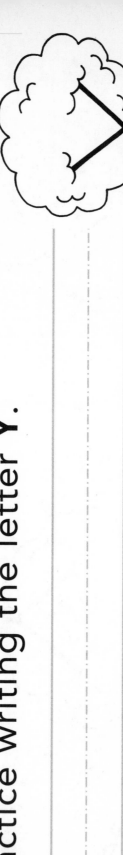

7. Practice writing words with **Y**.

Yes

You

Diagonal Letters

Practice printing the letters with diagonals.

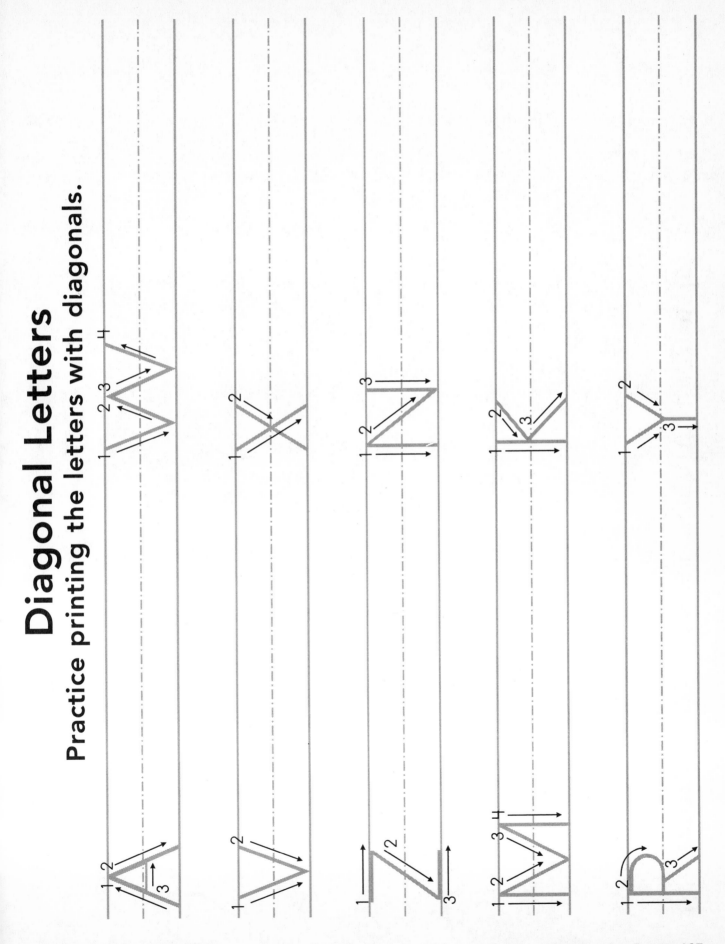

Practice printing the words with diagonals.

MAN

RAY

AX

WARM

VAN

Scholastic Professional Books